Knit BLANKETS&THROWS
with Mademoiselle Sophie

Mademoiselle Sophie of
Breaking the wool

Paris – San Francisco

STACKPOLE BOOKS
Guilford, Connecticut

© LIBELLA, Paris, 2015

This translation of *Plaids & Cie à Tricoter* first published in France by LIBELLA under the imprint LTA in 2015 is published by arrangement with Silke Bruenink Agency, Munich, Germany.

Translation copyright © 2017 by Stackpole Books
An imprint of Globe Pequot.
Distributed by National Book Network
800-462-6420   www.rowman.com

Editorial direction: Anne-Sophie Pawlas
Editing: Isabelle Riener
Proofreading: Valérie Balland
Graphic design: Anne Bénoliel-Defréville
Pagination: Coline de Graaff
Cover design: Tessa J. Sweigert
Photography: Claire Curt
Styling: Sonia Lucano
Production: Géraldine Boilley-Hautbois, Louise Martinez
Translation: Nancy Gingrich

First edition

Printed in the United States of America

British Library Cataloguing in Publication Information Available

Library of Congress Cataloging-in-Publication Data is available.
ISBN 978-0-8117-1791-5

Preface

The purpose of my first book, *Stylish Knit Scarves & Hats with Mademoiselle Sophie*, was to arouse your natural abilities and awaken (or reveal!) the sleeping but dynamic knitter within. Your many enthusiastic reactions, your messages of encouragement, and the many projects proudly shared on social networks filled me with happiness and gave me the energy to write a new chapter to this story.

For this book, I wanted to envision beautiful skeins of yarn in a setting that is particularly dear to me: the home. Because for me, a beautiful home has never been a matter of size. A beautiful home is a space in which you feel good, one that successfully balances the aspect of being enveloped by a sense of warmth and personal comfort with that of being open to others, a space conducive to interactions, discussions, to good times shared together. It's a home that is cozy and friendly. This principle guided my inspiration in designing and creating throws and blankets.

Throws are so soft to curl up in with a good cup of tea, but they are also superb decorating accessories, perfect to enhance a room, embellish a bedspread, or dress up a sofa with interwoven designs and pops of color.

Beginners or intermediates, this book has something for everyone, including explanations for techniques ranging from the garter stitch to lace patterns to cables stitches. No one will want to leave your "home sweet home."

I hope there will continue to be more of you who share my passion.

Mlle Sophie

Contents

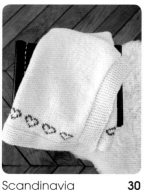

Materials

❖ Yarn

Use natural yarn such as wool, alpaca, or cashmere when possible; but you can also use wool-acrylic or wool-mohair blends. Your choice of yarn depends on the project you're making, and is very important. Make it a priority to use materials that are soft and pleasant to work with; it will be so much more enjoyable to knit with them and wrap yourself up in them!

❖ Needles

Needles in sizes US 7 (4.5 mm), 8 (5 mm), 9 (5.5 mm), 10 (6 mm), 10½ (7 mm), 11 (8 mm), 13 (9 mm), 17 (12 mm), and 35 (20 mm) are used for the patterns in this book. A wide selection of knitting needles is available. I prefer bamboo, but needles also come in metal, plastic, and wood. Each kind of needle has its own feel, depending on the material. Try several different kinds to find out which you like best.

❖ Circular needles

It is much more comfortable and convenient to knit large throws and blankets with circular needles rather than straight needles. Circulars are essential for pieces with a large number of stitches that cannot fit on regular needles. Very practical, they allow you to bring your knitting with you, thanks to the cable in the middle which bends easily.

There are two types of circular needles:
- fixed, with different cable lengths
- interchangeables, with cables that unscrew using a little key. A cap can be screwed onto the cable, allowing you to set aside your work.

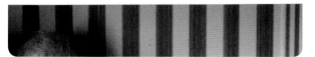

Knitting Lesson

CASTING ON

1. Make a slip knot, leaving a long tail of yarn, and place the loop around the needle. Wind the tail of the yarn around your left thumb, with the needle in your right hand.

2. Insert the point of the needle into the loop around your left thumb and, holding the needle with your left hand, wrap the working yarn (the end coming from the ball) around the point of the needle and draw it through the loop toward you.

3. Bring the loop over the point of the needle.

4. Gently pull down on the left end of the yarn: a stitch is formed on the needle. Repeat steps 2 to 4 until you have the number of stitches called for in the pattern.

KNITTING

1. With the work in your left hand and the yarn to the back, wrap the yarn around your right index finger. Insert the right needle into the first stitch, going under the left needle.

2. Wrap the yarn around the right needle, from bottom to top.

3. Slide the right needle down slightly, bringing the point through the stitch and back to the top of the left needle.

4. Slip the loop you just knit through off the left needle. You have just created one new stitch on the right needle.

5. Repeat the process, stitch after stitch, until all the stitches from the left needle are moved to the right needle; this creates one new row of stitches.

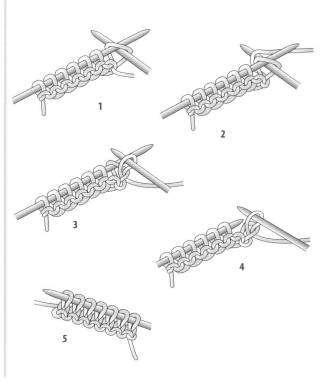

PURLING

1. Start with the yarn in front of your work. Insert the right needle into the first stitch on the left needle, with the right needle going in front of the left.

2. Wrap the yarn around the right needle.

3. Slide the right needle back underneath the left needle.

4. Gently pull the left needle to drop the loop from it. You have created one new stitch on the right needle.

5. Repeat the process, stitch after stitch, until all the stitches from the left needle are moved to the right needle; this creates one new row of stitches.

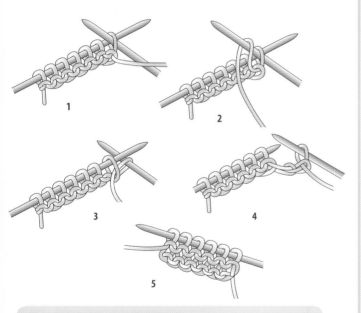

GAUGE SWATCH

Making a gauge swatch is essential for avoiding unpleasant surprises. A project may come out a very different size, your knit fabric may end up loose (because a smaller needle would have worked better with the yarn), or a neckline may end up too tight, depending on how tight you knit. Only a gauge swatch will ensure your project matches the original design. If your sample swatch is larger than the given dimensions, use needles one size smaller; if the swatch is too small, try one size bigger.

STOCKINETTE STITCH

Row 1: Knit every stitch.
Row 2: Purl every stitch.
Return to Row 1 and continue to repeat these 2 rows.

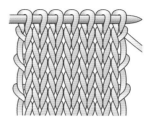

GARTER STITCH

Knit every row.

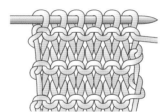

1X1 RIBBING

Row 1: Alternate one knit stitch and one purl stitch, being careful to hold the yarn at the back of the work for a knit stitch and to bring it to the front for a purl stitch.

For the following rows, work each stitch as it appears: knit into knit stitches and purl into purl stitches.

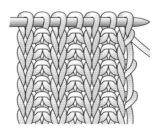

SEED STITCH

Row 1: Alternate one knit stitch and one purl stitch (as with 1x1 ribbing, remember to bring the yarn to the front or the back, depending on the stitch you're knitting).

Row 2: Purl into the knit stitches and knit into the purl stitches.

Return to Row 1 and continue to repeat these two rows.

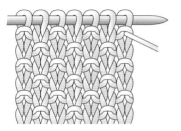

KNIT 2 STITCHES TOGETHER

Insert the right needle into the second stitch on the left needle, then through the first stitch as well; then wrap the working yarn around the needle and pull it back through the two stitches at the same time, just as if you were only knitting one single stitch.

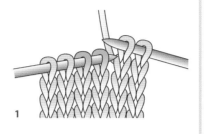

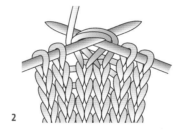

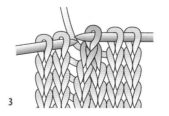

YARN OVER

This stitch is used to form a small hole. Bring the working yarn over the right needle without knitting it (1), then knit the next stitch as normal (2). This creates one extra stitch (3). To keep the number of stitches the same, knit two stitches together or work a slip, knit, pass (skp).

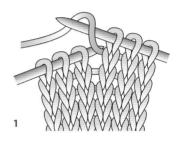

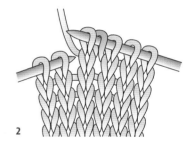

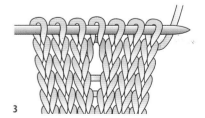

10

SLIP STITCH

With yarn in back, insert the right needle into the first stitch on the left needle, then slide it onto the right needle without knitting it.

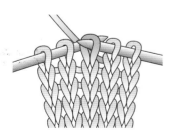

SLIP, KNIT, PASS

Slip one stitch knitwise onto the right needle (1), knit the next stitch, then pass the slipped stitch over the knit stitch (2). You will have one less stitch (3).

SIMPLE DECREASES OF 1 STITCH AT THE EDGES

Work two stitches together, depending on the type of stitch they are: knit two knit stitches together or purl two purl stitches together.

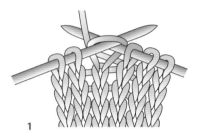

1

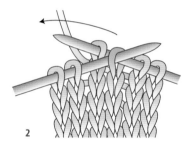

2

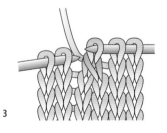

3

MAKE ONE INCREASES

When working make one increases, pay attention to the slant—first make one right, then make one left—for each group of increases.

- **Make one right:** With the right needle, lift the bar of yarn between two stitches (1) and place it over the left needle (2) from front to back. Then insert the right needle into the front leg of the yarn you just placed over the left needle, twisting it. Wrap the working yarn over the right needle and knit the stitch. You have created one new stitch, slanted to the right.

- **Make one left:** With the right needle, lift the bar of yarn between two stitches and place it over the left needle from back to front. With the right needle behind the left needle, insert it into the back leg of the yarn you just placed over the left needle. Wrap the working yarn over the right needle and knit the stitch. You have created one new stitch, slanted to the left.

BINDING OFF

Knit the first two stitches, then insert the left needle into the first stitch, lifting this stitch over the second one (1) and off the needle. Knit a third stitch and insert the left needle into the second stitch on the right needle and lift it over the third stitch and off the needle. Knit one stitch at a time, binding off the previous stitch remaining on the right needle by lifting it over the stitch just knit. At the end of the row, there will be one stitch left; cut the yarn, bring it through the loop and pull gently to tighten (2).

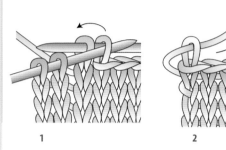

1

2

SEAMING

For a nice, finished look and invisible seams, first iron the pieces to flatten the edges. Place them next to each other, right side up, and insert a tapestry needle under the horizontal bar of the selvedge stitch on the first piece, then under the corresponding horizontal bar of the selvedge stitch on the second piece. Pull gently, bringing the two pieces together to obtain an invisible seam. Continue in this manner until the seam is finished.

Right

1

2

Left

1

2

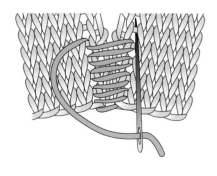

FAIR ISLE AND INTARSIA KNITTING

Fair Isle (also known as stranded knitting) is knit in stockinette stitch using two or more colors of yarn to create patterns, following a chart.

Each time the color is changed, catch the yarn on the back side of the work (crossing the yarn you drop with the new yarn) to avoid a hole; continue to cross the yarn each time the color is changed, on every row.

For small areas of color (a few stitches), the yarn not being used can be carried on the wrong side of the knitting, being careful not to pull it too tightly to prevent puckering. When you have a longer length of one color before changing to another, to keep it from hanging loose on the wrong side, cross the non-working yarn(s) with the working yarn about every 4 to 6 stitches to secure it on the wrong side.

When there are long intervals between color changes, I would advise you to work intarsia, using a separate ball of yarn for each color change, always crossing the yarns during color changes to avoid excess thickness and to save yarn. Bobbins holding small lengths of yarn can be helpful when working intarsia; you can buy bobbins, or make your own using a piece of cardboard.

TIP

Preferably use the same type and weight of yarn and, unless you are an experienced knitter, do not use more than three colors of yarn in one row.

READING CHARTS

A pattern with a colorwork design always comes with a chart. It may be black and white with a symbol for each color, or in color with the colors used in the motifs. Charts are read from right to left (right side rows in knit stitch) and left to right (wrong side rows in purl stitch), as well as from bottom to top in the same sense as the work. Here are two examples of charts using symbols and colors (both show the same motif).

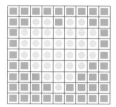

☐ Blue
○ Yellow

■ Blue
● Yellow

TIP

The front side of Fair Isle knitting must be very even, with all stitches the same size for the entire row. Each time the color is changed, be sure to cross the yarns, and be careful to make the last stitch made in the previous color and the first stitch knit in the next color neither too loose nor too tight.

BLOCKING YOUR WORK

When an item is completed, blocking will give it a good finish. The piece will be flattened slightly and some stitches, such as ribbing and cables, will stand out more. Iron all pieces on the wrong side and at a low temperature. If some edges have a tendency to curl, iron them a second time, very gently, on the right side. Then assemble the whole item.

16

ABBREVIATIONS

We have used the following abbreviations in this book to allow you to quickly and easily read the instructions.

Decrease(s)	*dec(s)*
Increase(s)	*inc(s)*
Knit 2 stitches together	*k2tog*
Knit	*k*
Make one	*M1*
Purl 2 stitches together	*p2tog*
Purl	*p*
Right side	*RS*
Slip, knit, pass	*skp*
Stitch(es)	*st(s)*
Wrong side	*WS*
Yarn over	*yo*

SOME TIPS

- **To start a skein,** it is best to use the end of the yarn found on the outside of the skein for fine yarns, and the end from the inside of the skein for thicker yarns; this way the skein will unwind easily. To switch to a new ball of yarn, join the new yarn over three stitches near the edge. Knit with the old yarn and the new yarn at the same time. Above all, don't make a knot.

- **To achieve an even knit,** practice on smaller pieces (doll scarves or squares for a small blanket). The yarn must be knitted smoothly—not too loose, not too tight—so the stitches will slide easily along your needles.

- **For attractive edges,** always tighten the yarn a little more on the first stitch; this way the knitting won't loosen as easily.

- **To pick up a dropped stitch,** insert the tip of a crochet hook into the dropped stitch, catch the horizontal strand of yarn just above it, and pull it through the stitch. Repeat for as many rows as the stitch unraveled, then replace the stitch on the left needle.

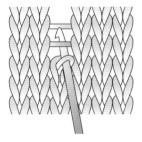

SKILL LEVEL

✳ *EASY*

✳✳ *INTERMEDIATE*

✳✳✳ *ADVANCED*

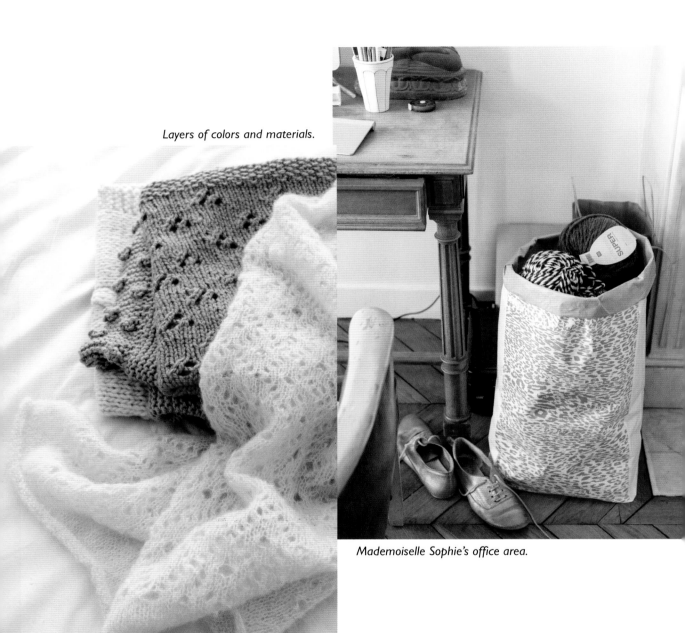

Layers of colors and materials.

Mademoiselle Sophie's office area.

Karma the cat is never far away.

Combination of various stitches.

Plumetis *

Stars seem to have rained down on this beautiful midnight blue throw.

MATERIALS

* *Aran weight yarn, approximately 10.5 oz./ 300 g, in navy blue (4 skeins) and white (2 skeins); shown in Fonty Numéro 5 (100% wool), #212 and #206*
* *Size 9 (5.5 mm) needles*
* *1 yarn needle*

STITCHES USED

* *Stockinette stitch*
* *Seed stitch*
* *Fair Isle*

GAUGE

* *In stockinette stitch with size 9 needles: 4" x 4"/10 x 10 cm = 15 sts x 19 rows*

SIZE

* *28" x 28"/70 x 70 cm*

Cast on 112 sts.

Rows 1 to 10: Work in seed stitch (to make the border).

Row 11: 5 sts in seed stitch, knit to last 5 sts, 5 sts in seed stitch.

Row 12: 5 sts in seed stitch, purl to last 5 sts, 5 sts in seed stitch.

Row 13: Begin the plumetis pattern, following the chart, remembering to knit the first and last 5 stitches of each row in seed stitch.

Continue until the throw measures 26"/66 cm, ending with a purl row.

End with 10 rows of seed stitch. Bind off.

Weave in ends.

I knit, navy blue yarn

— purl, navy blue yarn

▪ knit, white yarn

Berlingot **

An ultra-smart throw: light pink for tenderness and fuchsia for cheerfulness!

MATERIALS

❋ Super bulky weight yarn, approximately 21 oz./600 g, in fuchsia and light pink (6 skeins of each); shown in Fonty Pole (65% wool, 35% alpaca), #386 and #369
❋ Size 11 (8 mm) needles
❋ 1 yarn needle

STITCHES USED

❋ Garter stitch
❋ Make one increase
❋ Knit 2 together decrease

GAUGE

❋ In garter stitch with size 11 needles: 4" x 4"/10 x 10 cm = 10 sts x 21 rows

SIZE

❋ 35" x 35"/90 x 90 cm

Using color of your choice, cast on 3 sts.

Row 1: K3.
Row 2: K2, M1, k1.
Row 3: K3, M1, k1.
Row 4: K4, M1, k1.

Continue in pattern until the piece is approximately 24.5"/62.5 cm high. Change colors.

Knit 1 row in garter stitch with the new color.

Begin decreases: Knit each row in garter stitch until the last 3 sts, then k2tog, k1.

Continue in pattern until there are only 3 sts left.

Bind off.

Weave in ends.

Color Block ＊

A vibrant pink band brings style and energy to this striped garter stitch blanket.

MATERIALS

❊ DK weight yarn, approximately 21 oz./600 g, in dark gray (3 skeins), purple (3 skeins), mauve (2 skeins), pearl (2 skeins), and bright pink (2 skeins); shown in Fonty Gueret (100% wool), #004, #008, #019, and #027, and Bergère de France Barisienne (100% acrylic), #296-431.

❊ Size 7 (4.5 mm) needles

❊ 1 yarn needle

STITCH USED

❊ Garter stitch

GAUGE

❊ In garter stitch with size 7 needles: 4" x 4"/10 x 10 cm = 21 sts x 42 rows

SIZE

❊ 28" x 51"/70 x 130 cm

Cast on 145 sts with the purple yarn.

Knit approximately 12"/30.5 cm in garter stitch.

With the mauve yarn, knit approximately 9"/23 cm in garter stitch.

With the bright pink, knit approximately 11"/28 cm in garter stitch.

With the pearl, knit approximately 8"/20.5 cm in garter stitch.

With the dark gray, knit approximately 11"/28 cm in garter stitch.

Be sure you have about 4 yd./4 m of the dark gray yarn left, then bind off loosely.

Weave in ends.

Checkerboard *

An oh-so-soft blanket to tenderly wrap your baby.

MATERIALS

* Super bulky weight yarn, approximately 24.5 oz./ 700 g, in slate (7 skeins); shown in Bergère de France Galaxie 100 (80% acrylic, 18% wool, 2% polyester), #299-721
* Size 10 (6 mm) needles
* 1 yarn needle

STITCHES USED

* Garter stitch
* Stockinette stitch

GAUGE

* In garter stitch with size 10 needles: 4" x 4"/10 x 10 cm = 10 sts x 16 rows

SIZE

* 24" x 28"/60 x 70 cm

Cast on 60 sts.

Row 1: *K10, p10; repeat from * to end of row.

Row 2: Purl.

Work these 2 rows 8 times (16 rows).

Row 17: *P10, k10; repeat from * to end of row.

Row 18: Purl.

Work last 2 rows 8 times (16 rows).

Repeat Rows 1 to 32 until the blanket measures about 28"/71 cm.

After the 15th row of the last set of squares, bind off loosely.

Weave in ends.

Tweed **

Understated and elegant, this marl-like throw is so stylish.

MATERIALS

❈ Aran weight yarn,
  approximately 10.5 oz./
  300 g, in gray (4 skeins)
  and silver (2 skeins); shown
  in Fonty Numéro 5
  (100% wool), #227, and
  Rico Fashion Métallisé Aran
  (58% acrylic, 42% wool),
  #002
❈ Size 10 (6 mm) needles
❈ 1 yarn needle

STITCHES USED

❈ Garter stitch
❈ Fair Isle
❈ Stockinette stitch

GAUGE

❈ In stockinette stitch with
  size 10 needles:
  4" x 4"/10 x 10 cm =
  19 sts x 23 rows

SIZE

❈ 23" x 32"/58 x 80 cm

Cast on 103 sts with the gray yarn.

Knit 14 rows in garter stitch (2"/5 cm).

Row 15: K9 with gray yarn, *k1 with gray yarn, k1 with silver yarn; repeat from * to last 10 sts, k10 with gray yarn.

Row 16: K9 with gray yarn, *p1 with silver yarn, p1 with gray yarn; repeat from * to last 10 sts, p1 with silver yarn, k9 with gray yarn.

Repeat these 2 rows until the throw is approximately 30"/76 cm long.

Continuing to work in the gray only, knit 13 rows in garter stitch (2"/5 cm).

Bind off loosely.

Weave in ends.

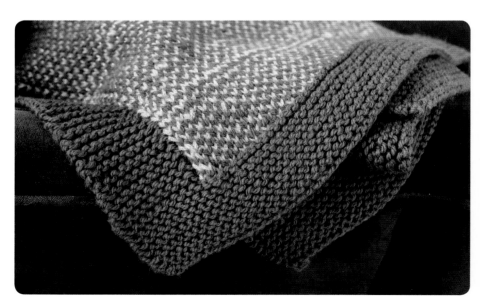

Scandinavia **

The spirit of Sweden shines through in this impeccable throw enhanced with a delicate border of red hearts.

Cast on 119 sts with the ecru yarn.

Rows 1 to 14: Knit in garter stitch (approximately 2"/5 cm).

Row 15: K9, p 101, k9.

Row 16 (RS): K9, k 101, k9.

Row 17 (WS): Repeat Row 15.

Row 18 (RS): Repeat Row 16. You will have approximately $3/4$"/ 2 cm of stockinette stitch on RS.

Row 19 (WS): Begin the Fair Isle pattern following the chart.

Work the next 7 rows of the chart.

Continue in stockinette stitch with the ecru yarn.

When the throw measures 28"/70 cm long, repeat the Fair Isle motif, following the chart.

Continue with the ecru yarn, repeating Rows 15 to 18.

Knit 14 rows in garter stitch (approximately 2"/5 cm).

Bind off loosely.

Weave in ends.

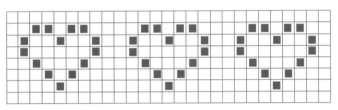

Tasseled Garter Stitch Throw *

I designed sizes for both mom and child. The neon tassels bring style and whimsy to these cozy throws.

MATERIALS

❋ Super bulky yarn, approximately 25 oz./700 g, in navy blue (adult size, 7 skeins) or 10.5 oz./300 g, in light blue (child size, 3 skeins), and neon pink for the tassels (1 skein); shown in Fonty Pacha (100% wool), #110 or #048, and Rico Essentials Big (50% wool, 50% acrylic), #026

❋ Size 17 (12 mm) needles

❋ 1 yarn needle

STITCH USED

❋ Garter stitch

GAUGE

❋ In garter stitch with size 17 needles: 4" x 4"/10 x 10 cm = 8 sts x 8 rows

SIZE

❋ Adult: 41" x 35"/ 105 x 90 cm
❋ Child: 22" x 17.5"/ 55 x 45 cm

Note: The numbers in parentheses are for the child's size.

Cast on 90 (45) sts, knit in garter stitch until the throw measures 41 (22)"/105 (55) cm.

Bind off. Weave in ends.

For both sizes, cut 16 strands of the neon pink yarn, approximately 10"/25 cm long.

Separate into four bundles of four strands each. Fold one bundle of strands in half, then pass the folded end through the stitches in one corner of the throw. Use your fingers to draw the free ends through the loop and pull gently to form the tassel. Repeat in the other three corners.

I Love Knitting **

Flaunt your addiction to needlework, especially knitting!

MATERIALS
❊ Super bulky yarn,
approximately 16 oz./450 g,
in white (1 skein) and
purple (8 skeins); shown in
Fonty Pole (65% wool, 35%
alpaca), #350 and #366
❊ Size 11 (8 mm) needles
❊ 1 yarn needle

STITCHES USED
❊ Garter stitch
❊ Stockinette stitch
❊ Fair Isle

GAUGE
❊ In garter stitch with
size 11 needles:
4" x 4"/10 x 10 cm =
11 sts x 19 rows

SIZE
❊ 28" x 30"/70 x 75 cm

Cast on 81 sts.

Rows 1 to 9: Knit in garter stitch.

Row 10: Knit.

Row 11: K6, p69, k6.

Row 12: Knit.

Row 13: Repeat Row 11.

Row 14 (RS): Maintaining the garter stitch border, begin the Fair Isle pattern, following the chart and placement you have chosen.

Once you have finished the Fair Isle pattern, repeat Rows 10 to 13 until the throw is 28"/70 cm long.

Finish by knitting 9 rows in garter stitch.

Bind off and weave in ends.

TIP
Experienced knitters may wish to design their own messages, creating a chart with words of their choosing.

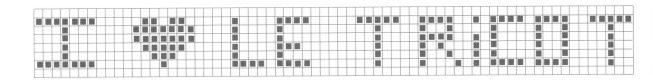

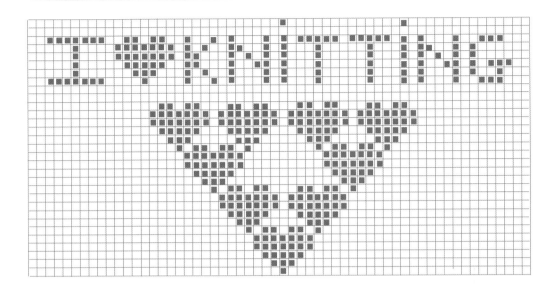

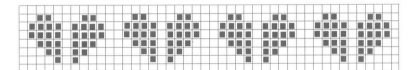

Super Chunky Throw *

Knit in rib stitch with oversize needles, this heavyweight throw shines in a spectacular red.

MATERIALS
* ❋ Super bulky yarn, approximately 18.5 oz./ 520 g, in red (6 skeins); shown in Rico Essentials Super Super Chunky (50% wool, 50% acrylic), #014
* ❋ Size 35 (20 mm) needles
* ❋ 1 yarn needle

STITCH USED
* ❋ 2x2 rib stitch

GAUGE
* ❋ In rib stitch with size 35 needles: 4" x 4"/10 x 10 cm = 4 sts x 6 rows

SIZE
* ❋ 43" x 39"/110 x 98 cm

This throw is knit with two strands of yarn held together.

Cast on 46 sts with the 2 strands of yarn.

Row 1: *K2, p2; repeat from * to end of row, then K2.

Row 2 and all remaining rows: Work the stitches as they appear (knit into knit stitches and purl into purl stitches).

Continue until the throw is 43"/110 cm long (approximately 66 rows).

Bind off. Weave in ends.

Soft Polka-Dots **

The large spots give a playful boost to the camel background.

MATERIALS

❋ Aran weight yarn,
approximately 12.5 oz./
350 g, in camel (5 skeins)
and dark gray (2 skeins);
shown in Fonty Numéro 5
(100% wool), #226 and
#238
❋ Size 8 (5 mm) needles
❋ 1 yarn needle

STITCHES USED

❋ Stockinette stitch
❋ Garter stitch
❋ Intarsia

GAUGE

❋ In stockinette stitch with
size 8 needles:
4" x 4"/10 x 10 cm =
18 sts x 23 rows

SIZE

❋ 26" x 26"/65 x 65 cm

Cast on 119 sts.

Knit 16 rows in garter stitch.

Next, continuing the border by knitting 9 stitches (garter stitch) at the beginning and end of each row, knit 5 rows in stockinette stitch. Then begin the color pattern following the chart, starting with a WS row.

When your piece reaches approximately 24"/60 cm, knit in garter stitch with the camel yarn for another 16 rows, then bind off loosely.

Weave in ends.

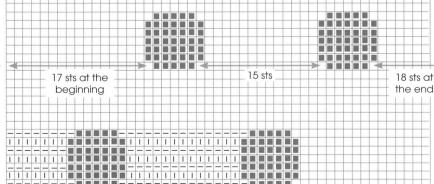

2nd row of dots, and all even rows of dots

17 sts at the beginning

15 sts

18 sts at the end

I knit, with camel

– purl, with camel

■ work in dark gray, knitting on RS and purling on WS

8 sts

15 sts

Neon Cat **

Brightened by a cat silhouette with a pop of neon, this soft little throw will make you purr with pleasure.

MATERIALS

❋ *Aran weight yarn, approximately 10.5 oz./ 300 g, in chocolate (5 skeins), ecru (1 skein), and neon pink (a few grams); shown in Rico Essentials Soft Merino Aran (100% wool), #054 and #60, and Phildar (acrylic), neon pink.*

❋ *Size 8 (5 mm) needles*

❋ *1 yarn needle*

STITCHES USED

❋ *Double seed stitch*

❋ *Stockinette stitch*

❋ *Fair Isle or intarsia*

GAUGE

❋ *In stockinette stitch with size 8 needles, 4" x 4"/10 x 10 cm = 20 sts x 26 rows*

SIZE

❋ *28" x 31.5"/70 x 80 cm*

Cast on 140 sts.

Knit as follows:

Row 1: K1, p1 to end of row.
Row 2: P1, k1 to end of row.
Row 3: P1, k1 to end of row.
Row 4: K1, p1 to end of row.
Rows 5 to 16: Work Rows 1 to 4 three more times.

Your work will be approximately 2"/5 cm high, then knit as follows:

Row 17: (K1, p1) 5 times, k120, (k1, p1) 5 times.
Row 18: (P1, k1) 5 times, p120, (p1, k1) 5 times.
Row 19: (P1, k1) 5 times, k120, (p1, k1) 5 times.
Row 20: (K1, p1) 5 times, p120, (k1, p1) 5 times.
Rows 21 to 24: Repeat Rows 17 to 20 (approximately 1.25"/3 cm of stockinette stitch).
Row 25: Continuing with the double seed stitch border and stockinette stitch, begin the Fair Isle pattern, following the chart (p. 45).

Once you have finished the charted pattern, repeat Rows 17 to 20 until the throw measures 30"/75 cm in all.

Next knit the border as follows:

Row 1: K1, p1 to end of row.
Row 2: P1, k1 to end of row.
Row 3: P1, k1 to end of row.
Row 4: K1, p1 to end of row.
Row 5 to 16: Work Rows 1 to 4 three more times.

Cast off loosely and weave in ends.

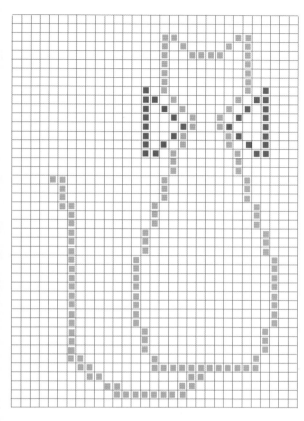

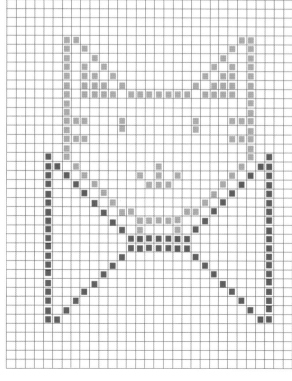

TIP

If you'd like, rather than just creating a silhouette, knit the entire cat in white yarn to create a very graphic image. Or try the chart at right for a close-up of the cat's face.

Sweet Ballerina **

Incredibly soft, this mohair throw brings to mind a ballerina's wrap sweater.

MATERIALS

❋ Sport weight yarn, approximately 7.5 oz./ 210 g, in light peach (5 skeins); shown in Fonty Ombelle (70% kid mohair, 25% wool, 5% polyamide), #1042
❋ Size 8 (5 mm) needles
❋ 1 yarn needle

STITCHES USED

❋ Knit stitch
❋ Purl stitch
❋ Yarn over
❋ Slip, knit, pass
❋ Knit 2 together

GAUGE

❋ In stockinette stitch with size 8 needles: 4" x 4"/10 x 10 cm = 14 sts x 18 rows

SIZE

❋ 43" x 37"/110 x 95 cm

Cast on 160 sts. Knit in stockinette stitch for 3"/8 cm.

Begin the lace pattern (the border is knit in stockinette stitch).

Row 1: K10, *yo, skp, k1, k2tog, double yo, skp, k1, k2tog, yo; repeat from * to last 10 sts, k10.
Row 2: Purl all except for double yarn overs; p1 and k1 into those stitches.
Row 3: K10, *k2tog, yo, k6, yo, skp; repeat from * to last 10 sts, k10.
Row 4: Purl.
Row 5: K10, *k1, k2tog, yo, k4, yo, skp, k1; repeat from * to last 10 sts, k10.
Row 6: Purl.
Row 7: K10, *k2, k2tog, yo, k2, yo, skp, k2; repeat from * to last 10 sts, k10.
Row 8: Purl.
Row 9: K10, *yo, skp, k1, k2tog, double yo, skp, k1, k2tog, yo; repeat from * to last 10 sts, k10.

Row 10: Same as Row 2.
Row 11: K10, *k3, yo, skp, k2tog, yo, k3; repeat from * to last 10 sts, k10.
Row 12: Purl.
Row 13: K10, *k2, yo, skp, k2, k2tog, yo, k2; repeat from * to last 10 sts, k10.
Row 14: Purl.
Row 15: K10 *k1, yo, skp, k4, k2tog, yo, k1; repeat from * to last 10 sts, k10.
Row 16: Purl.
Repeat Rows 1 to 16 to 4"/10 cm less than desired length.

Finish with 4"/10 cm in stockinette stitch. Bind off.

Weave in ends.

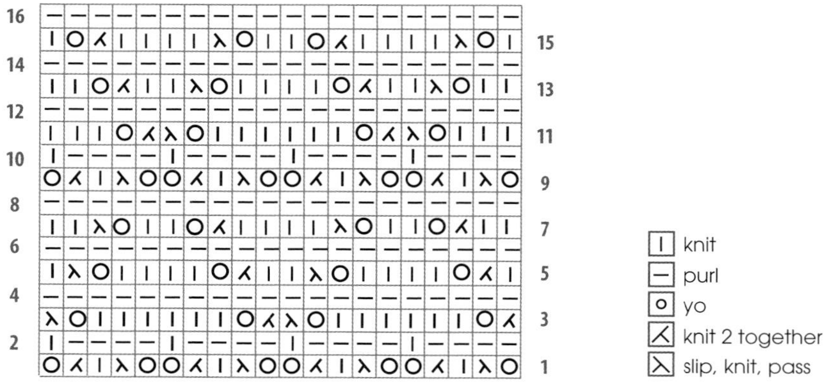

lace pattern

The diagram shows two lace pattern repeats.

I	knit
−	purl
o	yo
↗	knit 2 together
↘	slip, knit, pass

TIP

For knitters who are sensitive to the cold, this pattern can be worn as a scarf!

Provençal **

Rows of eyelets run along the width of this throw.

MATERIALS
* Aran weight yarn, approximately 13 oz./360 g, in almond green (8 skeins); shown in Fonty Numéro 5 (100% wool), #208
* Size 10 (6 mm) needles
* 1 yarn needle

STITCHES USED
* Garter stitch
* Stockinette stitch
* Yarn over
* Slip, knit, pass

GAUGE
* In stockinette stitch with size 10 needles, 4" x 4"/10 x 10 cm = 14 sts x 19 rows

SIZE
* 28" x 35"/70 x 90 cm

THE BORDER
Cast on 108 sts. Knit 14 rows in garter stitch.

Begin the eyelet holes pattern.

EYELET HOLES
Row 1: K10, purl to last 10 sts, k10.
Row 2: K10, knit to last 10 sts, k10.
Row 3: K10, purl to last 10 sts, k10.
Row 4: K10, knit to last 10 sts, k10.
Row 5: K10, purl to last 10 sts, k10.
Row 6 (RS): K10, *skp, yo; repeat from * to last 10 sts, k10.

Repeat Rows 1 and 2 for 2.5"/6 cm (about 12 rows).

Repeat Row 6 (the row of eyelet holes).

Continue repeating these 3 steps until your work measures about 25"/65 cm in all.

Knit Row 6 one last time.

Then repeat Rows 1–5.

Next, knit 14 rows in garter stitch to complete the border.

Bind off.

Weave in ends.

Patchwork **

Three different stitches plus two contrasting colors equal a strikingly graphic throw.

MATERIALS
❊ *Super bulky weight yarn, approximately 21 oz./600 g, in cinnamon (6 skeins) and white (6 skeins); shown in Rico Essentials Big (50% wool, 50% acrylic), #001 and #031*
❊ *Size 13 (9 mm) needles*
❊ *1 yarn needle*

STITCHES USED
❊ *Garter stitch*
❊ *Seed stitch*
❊ *Bobble*
❊ *Stockinette stitch*

GAUGE
❊ *In garter stitch with size 13 needles: 4" x 4"/10 x 10 cm = 10 sts x 20 rows*

SIZE
❊ *35" x 35"/90 x 90 cm*

TIP
Play with shades of colors to match the decor in your home.

This throw comprises four garter stitch squares, four seed stitch squares, and one bobble square.

WHITE GARTER STITCH SQUARE
Cast on 31 sts.

Knit in garter stitch for about 12"/30 cm.

Bind off loosely. Cut the tail of the yarn to about 16"/40 cm. It will be used to assemble the squares.

Knit 3 more identical squares.

CINNAMON SEED STITCH SQUARE
Cast on 29 sts.

Work (k1, p1) to last st, k1.

Work each row the same until the square measures 12"/30 cm.

Bind off loosely.

Weave in ends.

Knit 3 more identical squares.

CINNAMON BOBBLE SQUARE
How to knit a 5-stitch bobble:
Work into the same stitch 5 times, as follows: k1, p1, k1, p1, k1, then drop the stitch off the left needle and turn your work. Slip 1 and purl the next 4 sts. Turn the work, slip 1, and knit the next 4 sts. Turn the work, slip 1 and p2tog two times. Turn the work one last time and knit the last 3 sts together. Continue the row as it appears (knit) until the next bobble.

Cast on 29 sts.

Row 1: Knit.
Row 2: Purl.
Row 3: K4, *1 bobble, k4; repeat from * to last 5 sts, 1 bobble, k4.
Row 4: Purl.
Row 5: Knit.
Row 6: Purl.
Row 7: K2, *1 bobble, k4; repeat from * to last 2 sts, 1 bobble, k1.
Row 8: Purl.
Row 9: Knit.
Row 10: Purl.

Repeat Rows 3 to 10 until the square measures approximately 11.5"/29 cm.

Work 1 last bobble row, purl 1 row, then knit 1 row.

Bind off. Weave in ends.

ASSEMBLY
Follow the diagram (p. 55) showing placement of the squares. Sew them together with an invisible stitch using the white yarn.

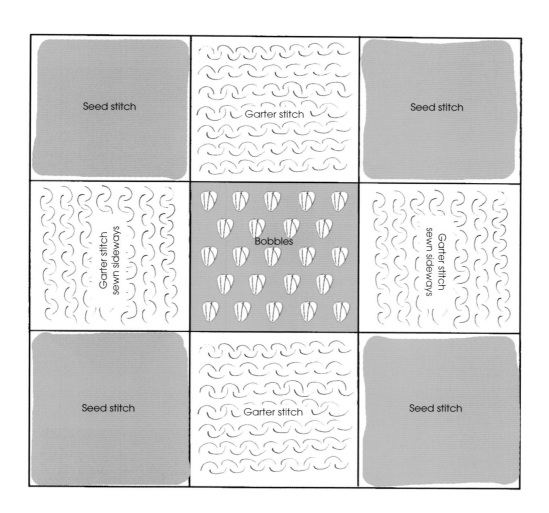

TIP

Feel free to change the order of the squares or to replace seed stitch squares with bobble squares to create a completely different look.

Brooklyn *

Delicately accentuated with vibrant pink stitches, this is a super soft throw to cuddle up with.

MATERIALS

❉ Bulky weight yarn, approximately 24.5 oz./ 700 g, in khaki (approximately 13 skeins) and neon pink (1 skein); shown in Bergère de France Mérinos Alpaga (60% wool, 40% alpaca), #29916, and Rico Essentials Big (50% wool, 50% acrylic), #026
❉ Size 10½ (7 mm) needles
❉ 1 yarn needle

STITCH USED
❉ Garter stitch

GAUGE
❉ In garter stitch with size 10½ needles: 4" x 4"/10 x 10 cm = 14 sts x 27 rows

SIZE
❉ 40" x 40"/100 x 100 cm

The blanket is composed of 25 garter stitch squares, sewn together with the same yarn. Once assembled, some of the seams are embroidered with a running stitch using the neon pink yarn (see photos).

THE SQUARES
Knit the 25 squares as follows:

Cast on 30 sts and knit until the piece is 8"/20 cm high (each square measures approximately 8" x 8"/ 20 x 20 cm).

Bind off and keep a yarn tail about an arm's length long to sew seams.

Assemble the squares, sewing together with an invisible stitch, then add the decorative stitching with the neon pink yarn.

Weave in ends.

Bobbles *

The luminous pearl gray and the three-dimensional border add elegance to this simple throw.

MATERIALS

❋ Super bulky weight yarn, approximately 30 oz./850 g, in pearl gray (17 skeins); shown in Fonty Pole (65% wool, 35% alpaca), #358
❋ Size 11 (8 mm) needles
❋ 1 yarn needle

STITCHES USED

❋ Garter stitch
❋ Bobble

GAUGE

❋ In garter stitch with size 11 needles: 4" x 4"/10 x 10 cm = 11 sts x 23 rows

SIZE

❋ 37" x 41"/95 x 105 cm

Cast on 90 stitches. Knit in garter stitch until the piece measures 35"/90 cm.

Bind off.

Weave in ends.

THE BORDER

How to knit a 3-stitch bobble:
Work into the same stitch 3 times, as follows: k1, p1, k1, then drop the stitch off the left needle and turn your work. Slip 1 and purl the next 2 sts. Turn the work, slip 1 and knit the next 2 sts. Turn the work, slip 1 and p2tog. Turn the work one last time and knit the last 2 sts together.

Cast on 10 sts and knit in garter stitch for 2 rows.

Row 3: K2, 1 bobble, k7.
Rows 4 to 9: Knit.
Row 10: K7, 1 bobble, k2.

Continue in pattern until the border measures 118"/3 meters. Try the fit around your blanket and adjust the length as needed before you bind off.

Bind off.

Weave in ends.

FINISHING

Sew the border on all around the rectangle. Weave in ends.

58

TIP
Beginners may wish to knit the border in garter stitch, omitting the bobbles.

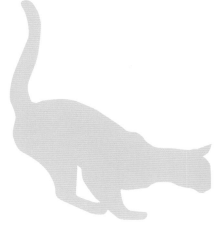

Cables **

Snuggled up with a book and the perfect throw to cover your knees = happiness.

MATERIALS

❋ Super bulky yarn,
approximately 23 oz./650 g,
in white (7 skeins); shown in
Fonty Pacha (100% wool),
#034
❋ Size 17 (12 mm) needles
❋ 1 yarn needle
❋ 1 extra knitting (or cable)
needle

STITCHES USED

❋ Garter stitch
❋ Stockinette stitch
❋ Cable stitch

GAUGE

❋ In stockinette stitch with
size 17 needles:
4" x 4"/10 x 10 cm =
8 sts x 12 rows

SIZE

❋ 39" x 45"/100 x 115 cm

Cast on 90 sts. Knit 5 rows in garter stitch.

Row 1: K5, k14, *p1, k6, p1, k14; repeat from * to last 5 sts, k5.

Row 2: K5, p14, *k1, p6, k1, p14; repeat from * to last 5 sts, k5.

Row 3: Same as Row 1.

Row 4: Same as Row 2.

Row 5: Same as Row 1.

Row 6: Same as Row 2.

Row 7: K5, k14, *p1, slip 3 sts onto the extra needle placed behind the work, k3, k3 from the extra needle, p1, k14; repeat from * to last 5 sts, k5.

Row 8: Same as Row 2.

Repeat Rows 1 to 8 until the work measures approximately 42.5"/108 cm.

Repeat Rows 1 to 6.

Then knit 5 rows in garter stitch. Bind off loosely.

Weave in ends.

RIGHT CROSS CABLE STITCH OVER SIX STITCHES

Place 3 sts on extra needle held behind the work, knit the next 3 sts, then knit the 3 sts from the extra needle. Knit the cable stitches normally in stockinette stitch. Cross the stitches at regular intervals.

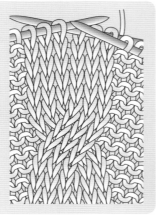

Romantic ✳✳✳

A throw that makes you want to curl up with a good book or take a nap.

MATERIALS

❋ *Bulky weight yarn, approximately 11 oz./310 g, in peach (7 skeins); shown in Bergére de France Alaska (50% wool, 50% acrylic), #299-477*
❋ *Size 10 (6 mm) needles*
❋ *1 yarn needle*

STITCHES USED

❋ *Seed stitch*
❋ *Knit stitch*
❋ *Purl stitch*
❋ *Yarn over*
❋ *Knit 2 together*

GAUGE

❋ *In stockinette stitch with size 10 needles: 4" x 4"/10 x 10 cm = 9 sts x 16 rows*

SIZE

❋ *31½" x 31½"/80 x 80 cm*

Cast on 74 sts and work 7 rows in seed stitch (beginning each row with a knit stitch).

Begin the eyelet pattern as follows:

Row 1: 5 sts in seed stitch, k4, *k2tog, yo, k8; repeat from * to last 5 sts, 5 sts in seed stitch.

Row 2: 5 sts in seed stitch, purl to last 5 sts, 5 sts in seed stitch.

Row 3: 5 sts in seed stitch, k3, *k2tog, yo, k2tog, yo, k6; repeat from * to last 6 sts, k1, 5 sts in seed stitch.

Row 4: 5 sts in seed stitch, purl to last 5 sts, 5 sts in seed stitch.

Row 5: 5 sts in seed stitch, knit to last 5 sts, 5 sts in seed stitch.

Row 6: 5 sts in seed stitch, purl to last 5 sts, 5 sts in seed stitch.

Row 7: 5 sts in seed stitch, k3, *k5, k2tog, yo, k3; repeat from * to last 9 sts, k4, 5 sts in seed stitch.

Row 8: 5 sts in seed stitch, purl to last 5 sts, 5 sts in seed stitch.

Row 9: 5 sts in seed stitch, k3, *k4, k2tog, yo, k2tog, yo, k2; repeat from * to last 8 sts, k3, 5 sts in seed stitch.

Row 10: 5 sts in seed stitch, purl to last 5 sts, 5 sts in seed stitch.

Repeat these 10 rows until the piece measures approximately 31"/78 cm.

Maintaining the seed stitch border, knit 1 row, then purl 1 row.

Work 7 rows in seed stitch.

Bind off.

Weave in ends.

	knit
	purl
	yo
	k2tog

Once again, none of this would have been possible without you, so I am extremely pleased to be able to thank you here.

Thank you to the entire team of Le Temps Apprivoisé and, in particular, to Anne-Sophie, Isabelle, and Stéphanie.

Thank you to the little fairy hands who held me up and helped me all the way along this adventure: Laétitia, Germaine, Martine, and Marianne.

Thank you to the entire team at Breaking the Wool: Julie and Valérie, my dynamic duo!

Thank you to the team at Ateliers Rrose Sélavy and, in particular, to Marie-Lorraine and Delphine for their support, their trust, and their cheerfulness.

Thanks also to Fonty (www.fonty.fr), Rico (www.rico-design.de), Bergère de France (www.bergeredefrance ,com), and Tulip (www.en.tulip-japan.co.jp) for their generosity.

Thanks also go to:

Marie from *Aime comme Marie*, for the animal print silk-screened brown paper bag, seen on p. 17 (www.aimecommemarie.com/)

Margot de Saisons, for the "James" wall hanging seen on p. 27 (www.saisons-lafabrique.com/)

Apple, for the Urbanwalls stickers, seen on p. 27

Maileg, for the cuddly polka-dot deer doll, seen on p. 53

Des Bulles Dans Les Branches, for the bouquets of flowers (www.desbullesdanslesbranches.com)

And finally, thank you to my whole family, my parents, my brothers, and, in particular, my husband and my two little angels to whom I dedicate this book.